God's Battle Plan for Purity

Strategies for Victory against Sexual Temptation

The Bible Teacher's Guide

Gregory Brown

Publishing

Copyright © 2015 Gregory Brown

The primary Scriptures used are New International Version (1984) unless otherwise noted. Other versions include English Standard Version, New Living Translation, and King James Version.

Holy Bible, New International Version ®, NIV® Copyright © 1973, 1978, 1984 by Biblica, Inc. ® Used by permission. All rights reserved worldwide.

Scripture quotations marked (ESV) are from The Holy Bible, English Standard Version® (ESV®) Copyright © 2001 by Crossway, a publishing ministry of Good News Publishers. All rights reserved.

Scripture quotations marked (NLT) are taken from the Holy Bible, New Living Translation, copyright © 1996, 2004, 2007 by Tyndale House Foundation. Used by permission of Tyndale House Publishers, Inc., Carol Stream, Illinois 60188. All rights reserved.

Scripture quotations marked KJV are from the King James Version of the Bible.

All *emphases* in Scripture quotations have been added.

Published by BTG Publishing all rights reserved.

Endorsements

"Expositional, theological, and candidly practical! I highly recommend *The Bible Teacher's Guide* for anyone seeking to better understand or teach God's Word."

—Dr. Young–Gil Kim, Founding President of Handong Global University

"Helpful to both the laymen and the serious student, *The Bible Teacher's Guide,* by Dr. Greg Brown, is outstanding!"

—Dr. Neal Weaver, President of Louisiana Baptist University

"Whether you are preparing a Bible study, a sermon, or simply wanting to dive deeper into a personal study of God's Word, these will be very helpful tools."

—Eddie Byun, Author of *Justice Awakening*

"I am happy that Greg is making his insights into God's truth available to a wider audience through these books. They bear the hallmarks of good Bible teaching: the result of rigorous Bible study and thoroughgoing application to the lives of people."

—Ajith Fernando, Teaching Director, Youth for Christ; Author of *A Call to Joy and Pain*

"The content of the series is rich. My prayer is that God will use it to help the body of Christ grow strong."

—Dr. Min Chung, Senior Pastor of Covenant Fellowship Church (Urbana, Illinois)

"*The Bible Teacher's Guide* is thorough but concise, with thought-provoking discussion questions in each section. This is a great tool for teaching God's Word."

—Dr. Steve Pettey, Dean of Louisiana Baptist Theological Seminary

"Knowing the right questions to ask and how to go about answering them is fundamental to learning in any subject matter. Greg demonstrates this convincingly."

—Dr. William Moulder, Professor of Biblical Studies at Trinity International University

"Pastor Greg is passionate about the Word of God, rigorous and thorough in his approach to the study of it... I am pleased to recommend *The Bible Teacher's Guide* to anyone who hungers for the living Word."

—Dr. JunMo Cho, Worship Leader and Recording Artist; Professor of Linguistics at Handong Global University

"I can't imagine any student of Scripture not benefiting by this work."

—Steven J. Cole, Pastor, Flagstaff Christian Fellowship, Author of the *Riches from the Word* series

Contents

Preface...11
Introduction...13
Strategy One: Know Our Battle...19
Strategy Two: Count the Cost of Failure...23
Strategy Three: Declare War...27
Strategy Four: Guard Our Eyes...31
Strategy Five: Guard Our Ears...35
Strategy Six: Guard Our Mind...39
Strategy Seven: Guard Our Free Time...47
Strategy Eight: Guard Our Brothers and Sisters...51
Strategy Nine: Guard Our Marriage...57
Strategy Ten: Find Faithful Soldiers to Fight Beside...61
Strategy Eleven: Battle from Home ...67
Strategy Twelve: Declare Victory...71
Conclusion...77
Appendix 1: Walking the Romans Road...79
Coming Soon...87
About the Author...89
Notes...91

Preface

> And the things you have heard me say in the presence of many witnesses entrust to reliable men who will also be qualified to teach others.
> 2 Timothy 2:2

Paul's words to Timothy still apply to us today. We need to raise up teachers who correctly handle and fearlessly teach the Word of God. It is with this hope in mind that the Bible Teacher's Guide (BTG) series has been created. The BTG series includes both expositional studies and topical studies. This guide will be useful for personal devotions, small groups, and for teachers preparing to share God's Word.

God's Battle Plan for Purity: Strategies for Victory against Sexual Temptation can be used as a four-week to thirteen-week small-group curriculum depending on how the leader chooses to divide the intro chapter and the twelve strategies. Every week, the members of the group will read a chapter or more, answer the questions, and come prepared to share in the gathering. Each member's preparation for the small group will enrich the discussion and the learning. Another way to lead the group is for the members to read the chapter and answer the questions together during the small group and continue with the next strategy as time allows.

I pray that the Lord may richly bless your study and use it to build his kingdom.

Introduction

> For you know what instructions we gave you by the authority of the Lord Jesus. It is God's will that you should be sanctified: that you should avoid sexual immorality; that each of you should learn to control his own body in a way that is holy and honorable, not in passionate lust like the heathen, who do not know God
> 1 Thessalonians 4:2-5

Purity is a raging battle that, unfortunately, many are losing. David lost this battle as he committed adultery with Bathsheba. Solomon lost it as he had 1,000 wives and concubines to fulfill his lust. If we are going to win this battle, we must be strategic and disciplined. Winning is important to protect our lives, our families, and our churches, and most importantly to honor God.

How can we keep ourselves pure? How can we win the battle for purity?

In 1 Thessalonians 4:2-5, Paul writes to the Thessalonian church and tells them to "avoid sexual immorality." Similarly, in 1 Corinthians 6:18, Paul said, "Flee from sexual immorality. All other sins a man commits are outside his body, but he who sins sexually sins against his own body."

This is startling because with many other dangers in Scripture, we don't get such a command. In

James 4:7, we are told to "resist the devil" and he will flee from us. In Ephesians 6:12 Paul says that believers "wrestle" against powers and principalities which refers to demons. With Satan and demons, we resist and wrestle, but when it comes to sexual immorality, we should avoid it and flee from it.

This demonstrates how dangerous sexual immorality is. When Joseph was tempted by Potiphar's wife to commit adultery, he jumped out of the window to escape her. It is the same for us. This is a danger that we should not flirt with, enjoy on our TV, or fantasize about. It is something that we must flee from at all cost.

It is for this reason that many stumble in this area and find themselves bound and unable to be set free. Sexual immorality is dangerous because when we commit sexual immorality, we sin against our own bodies. This sin affects one's mind, body, spirit, and emotions. It can have drastic effects. It opens the door for physical disease and emotional baggage. It can even affect one's sexual orientation. Those who have been sexually abused often grow up with perverse tendencies, whether that be towards the opposite sex or even children. Sexual immorality destroys homes, careers, friendships, and even one's faith. It is so hazardous that our only recourse is to flee from it.

One might ask, "If it's so dangerous why did God create it?" When God created everything, including sex, he said it was "good." However, when the world was perverted by sin, sex gained the potential of being destructive. In the confines of a marriage relationship—fulfilling God's original plan—sex is good and powerful. It creates intimacy and pleasure between a husband and wife and has the ability to lead to procreation. However, outside of that, it is destructive. In fact, Romans 1 says that one of the primary results of denying God is a distorted sexuality. When a nation, a community, or a person has turned away from God, it will typically be demonstrated through pervasive sexual immorality. Romans 1:22-24 says:

> For although they knew God, they did not honor him as God or give thanks to him, but they became futile in their thinking, and their foolish hearts were darkened. Claiming to be wise, they became fools, and exchanged the glory of the immortal God for images resembling mortal man and birds and animals and creeping things. *Therefore God gave them up in the lusts of their hearts to impurity, to the dishonoring of their bodies among themselves* (ESV)

This is what we are seeing and experiencing in today's culture and this is why it is such a battle. The world has denied God, and therefore, sexual immorality is rampant.

Problem in Culture

This was also true for the early church including the Thessalonians. The fact that Paul calls for the Thessalonians to "learn" how to control their bodies implies that many did not know how to control the lusts of their bodies (v. 4). Thessalonica was part of Greco-Roman culture in which sex was glorified. In that culture, when worshiping the false deities, one would have sex with the priests and priestesses (religious prostitutes) of which there were thousands. This was normal family life, as sex was part of worship.

For the Greco-Roman mindset, marriage was not the primary avenue for gratifying sexual desires; it was for social advancement and to provide an heir. By unifying two families, one could climb the social ladder. Thus, a beautiful daughter was like a meal ticket for a poor family. To fulfill sexual desires, it was quite normal and acceptable for a man to have mistresses and concubines. The gratification of sexual desires was not the focus of marriage in that culture.

Also, homosexuality and bisexuality were rampant in that culture. In fact, it probably would have been considered strange for a man to prefer one sex over another. It was considered normal to enjoy both.[1]

Problem in Church

The pervasive sexual nature of the culture was in the church, and therefore, the Thessalonians needed to "learn" how to control their bodies. This was also true for the church of Corinth which was also part of the Greco-Roman culture. In 1 Corinthians 6:15-16, the implication is that some were still having sex with temple prostitutes. Paul said this to them:

> Do you not know that your bodies are members of Christ? Shall I then take the members of Christ and make them members of a prostitute? Never! *Or do you not know that he who is joined to a prostitute becomes one body with her?* For, as it is written, "The two will become one flesh." (ESV)

In chapter 5, a man was even having sex with his father's wife (1 Cor 5:1). The world's sexual culture was in the church and they needed to learn how to keep their bodies pure.

Sex is also a problem for the modern day church. It is a problem for children, youth, college students, adults and even leadership, although it is rarely talked about. It is rampant. The enemy is aggressively attacking and defeating the church in this area. In the same way that sex was a problem in the early church, it is a problem for our churches.

In fact, in our culture, it may be even more pervasive. With the advent of the Internet, sex is more accessible now than in any other generation. At a person's whim, it can be watched on his or her phone at any moment. Statistics say that 70% of men ages 18-24 watch porn and one out of three porn viewers are women. The average age for a child to first view porn is eleven years old. [2]

Can we talk about sex? Can we talk about purity? If we don't openly talk about this in the church, as Paul did, we cannot conquer it. And sadly, a lack of addressing this subject seems to reap the most consequences on our young people, who are even more susceptible to the influence of sexual culture.

The enemy is bringing a great assault against the church today in the area of purity, and sadly like the Thessalonians and the Corinthians, the church is losing. To win this battle, we must develop a battle plan. Better yet, we must adopt God's Battle Plan in Scripture for purity. Through Scripture, God trains and equips the man of God for all righteousness—including purity (2 Tim 3:16-17). In this study, we will consider *twelve strategies* for victory against sexual temptation. May God thoroughly equip you to stand in this evil day. Amen.

Reflection

1. In what ways have you seen the sexual immorality in our culture become even more pervasive?
2. How would you rate your level of victory in the battle against sexual temptation from 1-10? And why?
3. Paul told the Thessalonians to learn to control their bodies and yet doesn't explain how. The implication is that they would learn from Scripture and the instruction of their leaders. What strategies have you learned that have helped in your fight to be pure?
4. What other questions or thoughts do you have about this section?
5. In what ways can you pray in response? Take a second to pray as the Lord leads.

Strategy One: Know Our Battle

In order to win the battle for purity, believers must first answer this question: "What is sexual immorality?" If we are going to avoid it and flee from it, we must know what it is. I think many Christians are failing simply because they don't know what sexual immorality is. It has never been defined for them. Some would even say that it is just "intercourse."

Many believe that oral sex, anal sex, masturbation, heavy petting, etc., are not part of sexual immorality. Such belief leads then to open these doors as avenues of fulfilling their lust while trying to maintain their "virginity."

However, by doing this, they are really committing sexual immorality and opening the door for the enemy to attack them and bring them under greater sexual bondage. Therefore, this is an important question to answer. What is sexual immorality?

In order to answer this question, let's consider 1 Corinthians 7:1-3:

> Now for the matters you wrote about: It is good for a man not to marry. But since there is so much immorality, each man should have his own wife, and each woman her own husband. The husband should fulfill his marital duty to his wife, and likewise the wife to her husband.

Paul, the author, said that it is good for a man to stay single and not marry. But because of temptation towards sexual immorality, each person should consider marriage as a spiritual protection. In marriage, the husband and the wife fulfill each other's sexual desires.

From this, we can gain this basic definition of sexual immorality: Sexual immorality is the attempt to fulfill natural sexual desires outside of the marriage union between a man and a woman. This includes things like sex, oral sex, anal sex, masturbation, heavy petting, pornography, and sexual imaginations. In short, sexual immorality encompasses all acts and thoughts designed to fulfill sexual desire outside of marriage.
In fact, Jesus said this about sexual immorality in Matthew 5:27-28: "You have heard that it was said, 'Do not commit adultery.' But I tell you that anyone who looks at a woman lustfully has already committed adultery with her in his heart." In other words, a person has already committed adultery when lusting, since he went outside of the marriage union to fulfill his sexual desires.

This might seem unrealistic to some. "How can anyone keep themselves from sexual thoughts?" And some might ask, "Why would they?" The reality is that God created sex and he has given us ethics for its use. If we pursue these desires outside the marriage union, we do it at our own peril. We sin against our own bodies, and most grievously, we sin against God.

How then should a single person respond to his natural desires? Scripture uses the analogy of sleeping for those desires. Listen to what Solomon's fiancée said in the Song of Solomon: "Daughters of Jerusalem, I charge you by the gazelles and by the does of the field:

Do not arouse or awaken love until it so desires" (3:5). She exhorts the young ladies in Jerusalem to keep their desires asleep until it is time.

Well, the next question we must ask is, "How can we keep those desires asleep?" or "How can we put them back to sleep after they have been awakened?" We will consider this in the following strategies.

Reflection

1. What was your previous understanding of sexual immorality?
2. Define sexual immorality. Why is it important to know its definition?
3. How commonly do you think people open sexual doors simply because of lack of truly understanding the definition?
4. Why is it important to keep sexual desires asleep?
5. When should churches and parents start instructing children about sexual immorality?
6. What other questions or thoughts do you have about this section?
7. In what ways can you pray in response? Take a second to pray as the Lord leads.

Strategy Two: Count the Cost of Failure

Just as with any battle plan, one must count the cost of failure. What will be the cost of being overcome by sexual temptation? We see this strategy used when Solomon counseled his son in Proverbs about the lure of the adulterous woman. Solomon, who had many wives and concubines, knew the consequences of sexual immorality well. His father's marriage began from an adulterous affair, and he struggled with his father's lust. Consider the costs of sexual immorality in Proverbs 6:27-35:

> Can a man scoop fire into his lap without his clothes being burned? Can a man walk on hot coals without his feet being scorched? So is he who sleeps with another man's wife; no one who touches her will go unpunished. People do not despise a thief if he steals to satisfy his hunger when he is starving. Yet if he is caught, he must pay sevenfold, though it costs him all the wealth of his house. But a man who commits adultery has no sense; whoever does so destroys himself. Blows and disgrace are his lot, and his shame will never be wiped away. For jealousy arouses a husband's fury, and he will show no

mercy when he takes revenge. He will not accept any compensation; he will refuse a bribe, however great it is.

Although Solomon is talking about adultery specifically, many of these consequences apply to lust in general. Solomon said, "Can a man scoop fire into his lap without his clothes being burned? Can a man walk on hot coals without his feet being scorched?" The answer to the rhetorical question is, "No!" In considering adultery, he said a person "destroys himself" and blows and disgrace will be his lot, and the shame will never be wiped away. The consequences last forever. Can anyone escape the penalties of indulging in lust? No. It is impossible. As mentioned, sexual immorality is a sin against one's body (1 Cor 6:18). It always affects one's body, mind, and spirit. It leads to mental and emotional baggage that is later carried into one's marriage. Personally, I still struggle with explicit images and thoughts from things I saw and experienced before marriage. I carry those as baggage with me from the sins of my youth. Sometimes, the consequences are physical sickness such as STDs. Other times, it is an unplanned pregnancy—potentially leading to an abortion. When married, the costs become greater. Marital unfaithfulness leaves brokenness and carnage in its trail. A brokenhearted spouse and emotionally damaged children are just a few of the consequences.

As a married pastor with a daughter, I always think of the consequences of falling to my lust. I think of the pain it would cause my wife, the destruction I would be raising my daughter in, believers who might fall away from Christ because of my example, and being disqualified from ministry (cf. 1 Tim 3:2, 1 Cor 9:27). The consequences would be devastating, and like Solomon said, the "shame will never be wiped away" (Prov 6:33). Certainly, forgiveness is available, but forgiveness does not eliminate the consequences. God forgave David for his adultery with Bathsheba and murder of her husband, but the consequences were the sword never departing from his home and losing his first child with Bathsheba (2 Sam 12:9-14).

Another consequence of sexual immorality that must be considered is its effect on our relationship with God. In the Beatitudes, Christ said, "Blessed are the pure in heart for they will see God" (Matt 5:8). The word "pure" means unmixed. When we allow lust and other wrong desires to enter our heart, it hinders our relationship with God. It separates us from him. David said, "If I had cherished sin in my heart, the Lord would not have listened" (Psalm 66:18).

Have you counted the cost of failure to sexual temptation? Fifty-six percent of divorce cases involved one party having an obsessive interest in pornographic sites.[3] The seeds cultivated in a man or woman's youth often bear destructive weeds in marriage. If we are going to win the battle against lust, we must count the cost. It is simply not worth it.

O Lord, keep us from dishonoring your name, damaging ourselves, and damaging others. Make our feet like hinds' feet and keep us from stumbling (Psalm 18:33). Create in us a clean heart, O God, and renew a right spirit within us (Psalm 51:10).

Reflection

1. What are some potential costs of falling into sexual immorality for both the single and the married?
2. How can considering the cost help in one's battle against sexual temptation?
3. Do you ever consider the costs of this battle? How has it helped? If not, why not?
4. What other questions or thoughts do you have about this section?
5. In what ways can you pray in response? Take a second to pray as the Lord leads.

Strategy Three: Declare War

The next strategy in God's Battle Plan for purity is identifying sexual temptations and being ruthless in getting rid of them. Listen to what Christ said in the context of teaching on adultery:

> If your right eye causes you to sin, tear it out and throw it away. For it is better that you lose one of your members than that your whole body be thrown into hell. And if your right hand causes you to sin, cut it off and throw it away. For it is better that you lose one of your members than that your whole body go into hell. Matthew 5:29-30

After teaching that a man who lusts after a woman who is not his wife has already committed adultery in his heart (v. 27-28), Christ says that one should be violent in removing temptations towards sexual sin.

The plucking out of one's eye and cutting off one's hand are hyperbole or symbolism for war time tactics. In ancient wars, when an army conquered another, they would at times pluck out the eyes and cut off the hands of the conquered so that they would never rise up and fight them again. This cruel tactic was used on Samson. When the Philistines defeated him, they blinded him with the intent of disabling him from ever harming them again (Judges 16:21).

By using this hyperbole, Christ shares how we must similarly declare war in order to be pure. He shows us how severely we must deal with sexual temptations. If our eyes—what we look at—are causing us to lust, we must get rid of it. If our hands—what we do—are causing us to sin, we must cut it out of our life.

The eye and the hand represent things dear to us—things that may seem essential for life. However, even these must not be spared in our efforts to be holy and pure. Is an intimate relationship tempting us? It must be severed. Is it our reading or TV watching? Let us discard it. We must be violent in our task of remaining pure and holy.

This violence will be demonstrated in various ways. I have had friends get rid of their TVs in order to be holy. Personally, as a seminary student and youth pastor, I wouldn't own the Internet at home because I wanted to protect myself from temptation. I would only use it at work or school. I even had to end relationships that went too far physically to protect the person and myself, but most importantly, to honor God.

With this said, we can understand why many cannot remain pure. The reason is simple. They just don't hate their sin enough. Purity is not a big enough priority to get rid of things that are dear to them. They love their eye and their hand too much. Friendships, TV shows, a dating relationship, the convenience of the Internet, etc., are too much to part with in their quest to be holy.

If we are going to win the battle against lust, we must declare war on it. Are you willing to go to war in order to be pure? For those who have opened sexual doors, this battle may be especially difficult and costly. But God will help as you are faithful.

Reflection

1. What types of cherished things commonly hinder a believer's quest for sexual purity? Why is it often so hard to let go of these things?
2. What things have you had to cut out of your life in order to be pure? Are there any things God is calling you to let go of currently?
3. What other questions or thoughts do you have about this section?
4. In what ways can you pray in response? Take a second to pray as the Lord leads.

Strategy Four: Guard Our Eyes

The next strategy in our battle for purity is guarding our eyes. Jesus said this, "The lamp of the body is the eye. If your eye is good your whole body will be full of light. But if your eye is bad, your whole body will be full of darkness" (Matthew 6:22-23).

What did Christ mean by the whole body being filled with light or darkness based on one's eye? In Scripture, light typically refers to what is righteous, good, and true, and darkness refers to what is evil, bad, and perverse (cf. Ephesians 5:9). To have a good eye means for a person to continually view what is godly, and therefore, a bad eye refers to continually viewing what is ungodly. Though the context of this passage is riches, it can refer to being filled with anything that is good or bad.

The eyes are a doorway to the mind and whatever one's mind continually thinks upon, a person will eventually do. If a person is going to be pure, he must be intentional about guarding his eyes. This will affect the types of movies watched, books read, and Internet sites visited. It will also affect how one looks at the opposite sex. For many, when they view the opposite sex, it is hard to not view them from a sexual standpoint. Their eyes continually trigger lustful thoughts and intentions, and if not combated, these eventually trigger lustful actions.

When a person views what is good or evil, it begins to "fill" them. To be filled means to be controlled by. In Ephesians 5:18, believers are called to be filled with the Spirit—controlled by it. When one is full of darkness, it means they are controlled by evil. In reference to lust, a person's lust can become out of control, even leading to tragic acts such as sexual harassment, rape, molestation, etc.

Sexual abuse statistics are frightening! One out of three American women will be sexually abused during their lifetime. One out of four women and one out of six men will be sexually assaulted by the age of eighteen. [4] Four out of five sexual assaults are committed by someone known to the victim.[5] Why is sexual abuse so pervasive and overwhelming? No doubt, it in part has to do with the increased access to erotic material in books, on TV, and on the Internet. The result of people viewing these materials is that eventually they can't control themselves—they are filled and controlled by the darkness their eyes continually engage in.

Conversely, a person whose eyes are continually engaging with the Word of God and godly things will be controlled by them. Fruits of the Spirit will be born in their lives—love, joy, peace, and self-control.

What are you filled with? Are you filling yourself with light which creates righteousness or darkness which creates uncontrollable, evil urges?

How can we practically guard our eyes?

Bouncing Our Eyes

Let's consider what Job said about disciplining his eyes. In Job 31:1, he said, "I made a covenant with my eyes not to look lustfully at a girl." In order to remain pure, Job guarded his eyes from looking at a woman lustfully. This was his continual discipline.

Some have called this "bouncing" one's eyes. When seeing an attractive female, instead of cultivating lustful thoughts and intentions, a man quickly bounces his eyes to something else. When seeing seductive images on the TV or the Internet, instead of taking a second look, one bounces his eyes by turning the channel or closing the webpage.

I remember one time in seminary seeing a young lady who was very attractive. I closed my eyes and prayed to God: "Lord, that woman is sooooo attractive—she will never get a second look from these eyes." This was the type of discipline Job implemented, and it is the type of discipline we must implement as well if we are going be pure. Remember Paul encouraged the Thessalonians to "learn" how to control their bodies in a way that is holy and honorable (1 Thess 4:4). No doubt, "bouncing" their eyes in a sexually charged culture was one of those disciplines.

How else can we guard our eyes?

Praying Over Our Eyes

Another discipline we should practice is prayer. David, a man who struggled with lust and pornography, often prayed over his eyes. In Psalm 119:37, he prayed this: "Turn my eyes away from worthless things; preserve my life according to your word."

He prayed for God to turn his eyes from the darkness of what is worthless to the light of God's Word. Whatever we practice becomes a habit. If we've practiced sizing up members of the opposite sex and looking at alluring images, then we will need even more grace to break those habits. Prayer is one of the ways that God changes our eyes from being dark to light.

Lord, turn our eyes from what is worthless to what is good.

Reflection

1. Why is it so hard to guard our eyes in this culture?
2. How is your struggle with your eyes? In what ways is God calling you to better guard them?
3. What other questions or thoughts do you have about this section?
4. In what ways can you pray in response? Take a second to pray as the Lord leads.

Strategy Five: Guard Our Ears

Another strategy we must implement is guarding our ears. Some might ask, "What difference does it make what we hear or listen to?" Consider what James said about the power of the tongue:

> Indeed we put bits in horse's mouths that they may obey us and we turn their whole body. Look also at ships: although they are so large and are driven by fierce winds, they are turned by a very small rudder wherever the pilot desires. Even so the tongue is a little member and boasts great things.
> James 3:3-6

By illustration, James describes how a powerful horse is controlled by a tiny bit in his mouth, and a ship is controlled by a tiny rudder. In the same way, the tongue, though seemingly insignificant, controls our lives. Whoever said, "Sticks and stones may break my bones, but words will never hurt me" was very wrong. Words are tremendously powerful. In fact, Proverbs 18:21 says, "The power of life and death is in the tongue."

Words spoken over a person's life has the ability to direct him—drawing him into a good and wise direction or an evil direction. It can build a person up or destroy him. If one sits under godly parents who faithfully teach God's Word and attend a good church that teaches the Truth, the "power of the tongue" will help direct him into what is good. But if one sits under ungodly teaching and ungodly conversations, it will affect his life negatively. This is especially true when it comes to sexual immorality.

No doubt, one of Satan's greatest tactics is to influence people sexually through the music industry. Much of today's songs are full of sexual overtones and graphic language. Some of it is essentially lyrical pornography—meant to control and guide people away from God and into sexual strongholds.

Sadly, many Christians fall prey to this tactic of the devil. They listen to ungodly, sexually charged music all day, then wonder why they can't control their lust and don't desire to read the Bible. The tongue is directing their lives—leading them away from God into lusts.

Psalm 1:1 says this: "Blessed is the man who walks not in the counsel of the wicked, nor stands in the way of sinners, nor sits in the seat of scoffers" (ESV). Some have called this the pathway of depravity. A person starts off listening to the "counsel" of the wicked, then he is standing in the way of sinners—practicing the same thing sinners do, and then they are in the seat of scoffers. Biblically, "scoffer" or "fool" is used of those who mock holy things. Psalm 14:1 says the fool says in his heart that there is no God. First, these people were just listening. Maybe like some Christians who listen to ungodly music, they say, "I only like it because of the beat; I don't even listen to the lyrics." The next thing you know, they are practicing sin, and one day they are mocking God and the practice of holiness. Satan led these poor souls astray by simply getting a hold of their ears.

In the same way, many raised in Christian homes with godly morals, such as waiting to have sex until marriage, are now sexually promiscuous just like the world. And it all started with the wrong counsel—sexually charged musical lyrics, sexual dialogue from movies, and sexually flirtatious conversations. Now, instead of following God, they mock what is holy and practice the sexual ethics of the world.

Who is speaking into your ears, and what are they saying? Are your conversations with friends full of sexual jokes and innuendo? Are your TV shows and movies promoting casual sex? If so, you won't be able to remain pure.

Paul said this in Ephesians 5:3: "But among you there must not be even *a hint of sexual immorality*, or of any kind of impurity, or of greed, because these are improper for God's holy people."

He said that there should not even be a "hint" of sexual immorality in our lives. Many desire to be pure but their mouths and the mouths of those they listen to are full of sexual hints that eventually bear fruit in their lives.

Are you guarding your ears? Satan keeps many Christians in bondage to lust by flooding their ears with sexual garbage.

Lord, help us to take out the garbage so we can be clean.

Reflection

1. In what ways does the enemy flood sexual temptation into our ears?
2. How have you seen or experienced the power of words, especially sexual words, in guiding one's life?
3. How is God calling you to better guard your ears?
4. What other questions or thoughts do you have about this section?
5. In what ways can you pray in response? Take a second to pray as the Lord leads.

Strategy Six: Guard Our Mind

Along with guarding our eyes and ears, we must also guard our mind. Consider what Paul said in 2 Corinthians 10:4-5:

> The weapons we fight with are not the weapons of the world. On the contrary, they have divine power to demolish strongholds. We demolish arguments and every pretension that sets itself up against the knowledge of God, and we take captive every thought to make it obedient to Christ.

Like Matthew 5:29-30, this passage uses warfare terminology for our battle against sin. In order to be holy and pure, both in heart and body, we must fight. War isn't easy. Our enemy is relentless in trying to conquer his prey, and lust is one of his most commonly used weapons. In this battle for our mind, Paul says we must "take captive every thought to make it obedient to Christ."

Satan always targets the mind—it is our primary battlefield. He bombards every believer's mind with sexual images and thoughts. He does this through the world system which he rules and his myriads of demons. He understands that if he can control the mind, he can control the body. So, if we are going to "learn to control our bodies in a way that is pure and honorable," (1 Thess 4:4) we must fight to control our mind.

Satan's attack on our mind overlaps with his attacks on our eyes and ears. It is through the eyes and ears that input is given to the mind. Therefore, by guarding the first two, we guard the latter. However, that is not the only way we guard our mind.

How else should we guard our mind?

1. In order to guard our mind, we must recognize ungodly thoughts and ideas by testing them against God's Word.

David said this in Psalm 19:7: "The law of the LORD is perfect, reviving the soul. The statutes of the LORD are trustworthy, making wise the simple."

The Hebrew word for "simple" has the meaning of "open-minded."[6] "The ancient Jews described it as someone whose mind was like an open door: everything went in and everything went out."[7] This person is gullible and will believe anything. His mind is open even to thoughts and images that should be rejected. However, David says that by filling the mind with God's Word, one becomes wise to discern what is not of God (cf. Heb 5:14). Wisdom in Scripture primarily refers to knowledge of God and obedience to him (cf. Prov 9:10). That is why Scripture describes the "fool" as one who says there is no God (Psalm 14:1).

A person who does not know the Word of God will have difficulty testing what is not good and therefore have difficulty protecting himself. His mind will continually be saturated by ungodly thoughts, sexual images, and lusts meant to control and destroy him. He will lack the power and discernment to close the door on sexual thoughts and many times will not only accept them but also cultivate them.

If we are going to protect our mind, we must recognize what is not godly. When watching TV shows, listening to music, or engaging in risqué conversations that cultivate and stir lust, the simple accepts what pollutes his soul, while the wise recognizes what would dishonor God's temple (1 Cor 6:19).

With all that said, guarding our mind does not stop at recognizing what is ungodly by testing it against God's Word.

2. In order to guard our mind, we must reject the ungodly by using God's Word.

While the simple opens the door, the wise closes the door. Again, this is done first by recognizing what is wrong and then using Truth to combat what is false and sinful. When Christ was tempted by Satan in the wilderness, he quoted Scripture to reject Satan and his lies. We should do the same. Arm yourself by memorizing Bible verses related to lust and purity such as:

> "You have heard that it was said, 'You shall not commit adultery.' But I say to you that everyone who looks at a woman with lustful intent has already committed adultery with her in his heart. Matthew 5:27-28 (ESV)

> Flee from sexual immorality. Every other sin a person commits is outside the body, but the sexually immoral person sins against his own body. Or do you not know that your body is a

temple of the Holy Spirit within you, whom you have from God? You are not your own, for you were bought with a price. So glorify God in your body.
1 Corinthians 6:18-20 (ESV)

For you know what instructions we gave you through the Lord Jesus. For this is the will of God, your sanctification: that you abstain from sexual immorality; that each one of you know how to control his own body in holiness and honor, not in the passion of lust like the Gentiles who do not know God; that no one transgress and wrong his brother in this matter, because the Lord is an avenger in all these things, as we told you beforehand and solemnly warned you. For God has not called us for impurity, but in holiness. Therefore whoever disregards this, disregards not man but God, who gives his Holy Spirit to you.
1 Thessalonians 4:2-8 (ESV)

Personally, when attacked by lust, I quote relevant Scriptures, confess wrong thoughts, lusts, and images before the Lord, and ask him to take them away. In our war for our mind, we must "take captive every thought to make it obedient to Christ."

3. In order to guard our mind, we may at times need to command the devil to leave in Jesus name.

Again, when Jesus was tempted in the wilderness, he initially responded to the temptation with quoting Scripture, but ultimately he commanded the devil to leave. Matthew 4:10-11 describes this:

> Then Jesus said to him, "Be gone, Satan! For it is written, 'You shall worship the Lord your God and him only shall you serve.'" Then the devil left him, and behold, angels came and were ministering to him.

Similarly, at times you may need to do this. When battles with lust, pornography, and illicit sex are especially difficult, we can be sure that the enemy has set up camp in these areas, and we may need to pray in authority over these demonic strongholds to be broken in the name of Jesus.

Some struggle with this, arguing that authority over the demonic was exclusively for Christ and his apostles. However, I believe there are many evidences that demonstrate this is for every believer. For instance:

- Christ is our perfect model for everything in life, including spiritual warfare (cf. Phil 2:5-11, Heb 12:2-4. 1 Peter 2:21-24).

We should model his life as the perfect example of humanity. His example in defeating the devil in the wilderness is not only descriptive but prescriptive.

- Other believers commanded demons to leave throughout the New Testament.

In Acts 16:18, Paul commanded a spirit of divination to leave a slave girl in the name of Jesus. And in Acts 8:6-7, Philip, who was possibly one of the early deacons, also cast out demons. Yes, Paul was an apostle but Philip was not. This was practiced by the early church.

- Finally, Scripture indicates that Christ has given us his authority based on our union with him.

Ephesians 1:20-22 describes his position of authority at the right hand of the Father seated above powers and principalities (the demonic) in the heavenly realm. And then Ephesians 2:6 describes how believers are seated with him. Again, this seating is not primarily a location but a position of authority which believers have in Christ. In fact, one day we will judge fallen angels with him because of this position (1 Cor 6:3). We have authority over the demonic just as the apostles and the early church, and we are called to conquer them with the spiritual weapons God has given us (cf. Eph 6:10-19).

Unfortunately, many believers neglect this authority not only to their own detriment but also to the detriment of others. When Christ sent believers into the world to proclaim the gospel, he sent them in all the authority given to him (Matt 28:18-20). We need this authority not just to spread the gospel but also for spiritual warfare.

Christ's authority is important in battling lust because some strongholds and temptations are not just of the flesh, they are demonic. Like Christ in the wilderness, Paul, at times, recognized certain obstacles and temptations were not just of the flesh and of the world, but of the devil. Paul said this in 1 Thessalonians 2:18: "we wanted to come to you—I, Paul, again and again—but Satan hindered us" (ESV). We need to discern this as well and resist the devil.

James says this: "Submit yourselves, then, to God. Resist the devil, and he will flee from you" (4:7). As we submit to God through his Word, prayer, and the ministry of other saints, we can resist the devil, and he will flee from us. However, at times, resistance may include commanding the demonic to leave in the name of Jesus as demonstrated by Christ and the early church.

It is not God's will for us to live bound to lust and sexual immorality, and God has given us all the resources to walk in freedom, including his Word and his authority. Thank you, Lord, for giving us everything needed for life and godliness (cf. 2 Peter 1:3). Thank you, Lord, for your grace. Thank you, Lord, that you are creating a pure and blameless Bride for your pleasure (cf. Eph 5:25-27).

Are you guarding your mind? Are you taking every thought captive and making it obedient to Christ? Are you filling your mind with God's Word? Are you resisting the devil's attacks so that he flees?

Reflection

1. Why is the mind so important in our battle for purity?
2. In what ways does the enemy bombard our mind with sexual images and thoughts?
3. How can a person tell when certain strongholds, especially sexual ones, are also demonic?
4. How should we resist the devil so he flees? In what ways is God calling you to better guard your mind?

5. What other questions or thoughts do you have about this section?
6. In what ways can you pray in response? Take a second to pray as the Lord leads.

Strategy Seven: Guard Our Free Time

The next strategy is guarding our free time. One of the major reasons people engage in sexual sins, such as pornography and masturbation, is simply boredom—not having anything else productive to do. The Bible seems to provide evidence of this. Unwise stewardship of time probably contributed to David's adulterous affair with Bathsheba. Consider the narrative:

> In the spring, at the time when kings go off to war, David sent Joab out with the king's men and the whole Israelite army. They destroyed the Ammonites and besieged Rabbah. But David remained in Jerusalem. One evening David got up from his bed and walked around on the roof of the palace. From the roof he saw a woman bathing. The woman was very beautiful, and David sent someone to find out about her. The man said, "Isn't this Bathsheba, the daughter of Eliam and the wife of Uriah the Hittite?" Then David sent messengers to get her. She came to him, and he slept with her. (She had purified herself from her uncleanness.) Then she went back home.
> 2 Samuel 11:1-4

In this story, the events occurred in the spring when kings typically went off to war; however, instead of going to battle, David sent the entire Israelite army while he stayed home. Next, David had a sleepless night and then decided to walk on the roof of his palace. While walking, he noticed a beautiful woman bathing. He saw, he lusted, and then he committed adultery with her.

Many men and women have had similar experiences. They were up late with nothing productive to do. They found themselves watching a show they shouldn't be watching, in a chatroom they shouldn't be in, on a website they shouldn't be on, or having a conversation they shouldn't be having. Like David, many are led into lust by not guarding their time.

There is more biblical evidence of the temptations associated with boredom. First Timothy 5:13 says this about widows and idleness: "Besides, they get into the habit of being idle and going about from house to house. And not only do they become idlers, but also gossips and busybodies, saying things they ought not to." Not having a husband leads the widows to idleness, and in turn, the widows become gossips and busybodies. There is a lot of truth to the saying, "An idle mind is the devil's workshop." When we have free time, it is often then that our enemy attacks. Loneliness, boredom, and procrastination are times when we are especially prone to lust, depression, addiction, and other temptations.

In addition, Paul says this in Ephesians 5:15-17: "Look carefully then how you walk, not as unwise but as wise, making the best use of the time, because the days are evil. Therefore do not be foolish, but understand what the will of the Lord is."

Why should we be careful to use our time wisely? Paul says because the days are evil—meaning that if we make poor choices with our time, there is a tendency to fall into the evil of the day. There is a tendency to fall into sin.

This is not only true about lust but any sin. When do people typically get drunk? In their free time. When do people typically struggle with pornography? In their free time. When do people indulge in addictions? In their free time. Satan realizes that our free time is prime real estate for temptation. Therefore, we must make the best use of our time.

In fact, "making the best use of the time" can be translated "redeeming the time" or "buying back the time." The word redeeming "was used of buying a slave in order to set him free."[8] We must redeem our time from the slavery of evil and instead use it for God.

How do we redeem our time and make "the best" use of it? Paul said that we must know and do God's will (v. 17).

For example, in the story of David's fall into adultery, he probably should have been at war instead of at home. As the king of Israel, he was called to fight the battles of Israel and to, specifically, conquer all of Canaan, as it was promised by God to Abraham's descendants. Therefore, during David's temptation, he was not using his time to do God's will—he was missing God's will. This is true for many Christians. Instead of using their time to get involved in church, small group, or youth group, instead of using their summer to grow in the Lord or do missions, they waste it and open doors to fall into the evil of the day. If we are going to walk in victory over lust (and any other sin for that matter), we must redeem the time and use it to know and do God's will.

How are you using your time? Are you redeeming it for God and his purposes? Or are you falling into the evil of the day?

Reflection

1. How have you found yourself more prone to lust and other temptations in your free time?
2. How can you better redeem your time and use it to do God's will?
3. What other questions or thoughts do you have about this section?
4. In what ways can you pray in response? Take a second to pray as the Lord leads.

Strategy Eight: Guard Our Brothers and Sisters

Another major reason Christians fall into immorality is because they have wrong ideas about dating and courting the opposite sex. Sadly, these relationships often model the world (Romans 12:2) instead of biblical principles.

Consider what Paul said to Timothy, a young single pastor in Ephesus:

> Do not rebuke an older man harshly, but exhort him as if he were your father. Treat younger men as brothers, older women as mothers, *and younger women as sisters, with absolute purity.*
> 1 Timothy 5:1-2

Essentially, Paul says that outside of marriage, one's interactions with the opposite sex should look like a natural brother and sister relationship. In fact, he says it should be identified by "absolute purity."

Again, most Christian dating relationships follow the pattern of the world. When I was a student, they called it first-base, second-base, third-base, and home. Couples went from holding hands, to kissing, to heavy petting, to sex.

However, Scripture presents a very different picture—a familial one. A dating relationship, in many ways, should resemble a sibling relationship. In considering Paul's teaching about relationships with the opposite sex, a man should ask, "How far would I go with my sister?" A fair application is if you wouldn't do it with your biological sister, then you probably shouldn't do it with your girlfriend. If you wouldn't kiss your sister, then you probably shouldn't kiss your girlfriend. If you go past the analogy given in Scripture, then you lose the witness of Scripture in your courtship relationships and the approval of God.

Once the boundaries of Scripture have been eclipsed, it is often like a slippery slope. First it's OK to hold hands, then it's OK to kiss, then it's OK to cuddle and touch one another, then it's OK to have sex because eventually you're going to get married anyway—one reasons. This is a pathway to destruction.

I always encourage couples to declare their boundaries when initially considering dating someone. If that person is not willing to keep those boundaries, then move on. It is a lot harder to pull somebody up, than to pull somebody down. In dating and courtship, it's important to be equally yoked, especially when it comes to purity.

A Warning about Clothing

In guarding your brother or sister, one of the things that must be considered is clothing. This is especially true for a woman since her body is more alluring than a man's. That is why in many cultures, it is socially acceptable for a man to have his shirt off and not a woman. It seems that God made the woman's body that way—it is the more delicate vessel (1 Peter 3:7). Also, this is especially important for women because men are typically more visually stimulated, while women are more emotionally stimulated.

In 1 Timothy 2:9-10, Paul said,

> I also want women to dress modestly, with decency and propriety, not with braided hair or gold or pearls or expensive clothes, but with good deeds, appropriate for women who profess to worship God.

This means that a Christian woman should avoid extremes in her clothing. She should not be known for dressing haggardly nor with expensive clothing, as is so common amongst the world. Peter, similarly, said this:

> Your beauty should not come from outward adornment, such as braided hair and the wearing of gold jewelry and fine clothes. Instead, it should be that of your inner self, the unfading beauty of a gentle and quiet spirit, which is of great worth in God's sight.
> 1 Peter 3:3-4

However, this modesty, especially, applies to provocative dress, which can cause others to stumble. It will be very hard for a woman to avoid provocative clothing, as Satan is the ruler of this world (John 12:31), which includes the fashion industry. Sex drives the fashion industry. Shorts and skirts continue to get shorter, tops reveal more cleavage, and pants are tighter. For a woman to dress modestly, she will have to go against the flow and be very strategic and particular in her purchases.

Dressing modestly is important to maintain purity and to protect a dating relationship. As a female, you don't want to open the door for the enemy into your courtship. Also, you don't want a man who is primarily attracted to you because of your figure. Solomon's mom said "charm" or "form" is deceitful, but a woman who fears the Lord is to be praised (Prov 31:30). You should want a man who is primarily attracted to you because of your love and obedience to the Lord, which includes modesty. Be careful of your clothing, as it can be a stumbling block to your brothers, and it will make it harder to stay pure in a courting relationship.

With that said, this is also true for men. Men need to consider their clothing in order to not be a stumbling block to their sisters. Men should be careful of wearing t-shirts that are 3X too small and pants with no air in them.

How is your clothing? Could it potentially be a stumbling block to others?

If you are going to win the battle for purity, you must guard members of the opposite sex by treating them as brothers and sisters with all purity and being modest in your dress.

Reflection

1. What are the common sexual practices of the world in regards to dating/courting?
2. What type of Christian instruction did you receive in regards to one's conduct in

dating/courtship relationships? What did that instruction include?
3. How would you apply Paul's exhortation to treat younger members of the opposite sex as siblings with absolute purity to dating/courting relationships (1 Tim 5:2)?
4. Do you feel as though Christian brothers and sisters often model the clothing standards of the world in regards to immodesty? How can we better hold one another accountable in regards to dress?
5. What other questions or thoughts do you have about this section?
6. In what ways can you pray in response? Take a second to pray as the Lord leads.

Strategy Nine: Guard Our Marriage

Many enter marriage thinking that lust will no longer be a problem; however, nothing could be further from the truth. Satan is even more diligent in attacking marriages because the consequences of failure are greater. Moral failure in marriage not only affects the husband and wife but also the friends, the extended family, the children, and the children's children. The consequences are drastic.

First Corinthians 7:2, 4-5 says this about sexual temptation in marriage:

> But since there is so much immorality, each man should have his own wife, and each woman her own husband.... The wife's body does not belong to her alone but also to her husband. In the same way, the husband's body does not belong to him alone but also to his wife. Do not deprive each other except by mutual consent and for a time, so that you may devote yourselves to prayer. Then come together again so that Satan will not tempt you because of your lack of self-control.

Paul teaches that sex in marriage protects from immorality. For that reason, married couples are called to faithfully serve one another sexually. When couples are not consistent sexually, it opens the door for Satan's temptations.

Here, I believe we learn something about Satan's strategy in the marriage union. Before marriage, Satan works overtime to tempt couples into "sexual intimacy," but in marriage, he works overtime to keep them from "sexual intimacy." The strategy changes. Often, right after the wedding, couples find it difficult to be consistent sexually. The husband and wife are often busy at work during the day, and in the evening, they are too tired to cultivate physical intimacy. Temptation to neglect the sexual union becomes even greater when children enter the picture. Couples tend to focus on their children to the neglect of marital relations. In some cultures, the wives co-sleep with the children for several years which also tends to hinder the frequency of sex.

This lack of consistency opens the door for Satan to attack the marriage in many ways. Sometimes, women feel unattractive and less desired by their husband, especially after having a baby. Insecurities begin to creep in and negatively affect the relationship. If the husband is neglected sexually, the enemy often tempts him to find pleasure elsewhere—whether through pornography or through an emotional or physical relationship with another woman.

One way for couples to be more consistent in the sexual union is to talk openly about it and plan for it. The fact that it is not spontaneous doesn't mean that it is not romantic. Just as in any area of life, "to fail to plan is to plan to fail." Proverbs 21:5 says, "The plans of the diligent lead to profit as surely as haste leads to poverty."

In marriage, couples protect themselves by faithfully practicing physical intimacy and closing the door on sexual temptation. In fact, Paul says if couples neglect physical intimacy, it should only be by mutual agreement for spiritual reasons—to fast and seek the Lord together.

Reflection

1. Why is it important for married couples to practice sexual intimacy?
2. What type of temptations does the enemy often bring when there is a lack of sexual intimacy?
3. How can married couples strategically cultivate sexual intimacy?
4. What other questions or thoughts do you have about this section?
5. In what ways can you pray in response? Take a second to pray as the Lord leads.

Strategy Ten: Find Faithful Soldiers to Fight Beside

Nobody fights a war alone—we need other godly soldiers to fight beside. Consider what Paul said to Timothy, "Flee the evil desires of youth, and pursue righteousness, faith, love and peace, along with those who call on the Lord out of a pure heart" (2 Tim 2:22).

Paul told Timothy to flee evil desires of youth, which refers to various ungodly desires including lust. We should find like-minded people of the *same gender* to fight beside—men with men and women with women. In a battle, the one fighting alone is the most vulnerable and susceptible to attack.

Why do some fight alone? Some fight alone because of shame—the enemy makes them feel ashamed of their sin. They feel like nobody else struggles with it, and therefore, they never tell anyone. However, Scripture says, "There is no temptation taken you but that which is common to man" (1 Cor 10:13). This battle is something that we all share to various degrees. Don't let the enemy lie to you and keep you from getting the support needed. Some fight alone because they think they can win the battle without help. However, 1 Corinthians 12:21 says, "The eye can't say to the hand, I don't need you." God created the body of Christ in such a way that we are interdependent—

meaning we need one another. We need one another to accomplish the works God has called us to do including gaining victory over lust.

Proverbs 13:20 says this: "He who walks with the wise grows wise, but a companion of fools suffers harm." Find wise, godly soldiers to pray with, to confess to, and to gain wisdom from in order to obtain and sustain victory against lust. These wise soldiers will include those who are battle tested and successful in winning the battle against lust. As a college student, I didn't really start getting victory until I began to be mentored and held accountable by an older, spiritually mature man. Previously, my accountability partners were primarily young men like myself who wanted to be pure but were losing the battle. This was not wrong, but it wasn't enough. Find wise, godly soldiers to help you win the victory.

In addition, it must be noticed that the companion of fools will suffer harm. This is also true in your battle against lust. If your intimate friendships and dating relationships are with individuals who are not zealous for righteousness and purity, their spiritual apathy and immorality will affect you negatively. Sometimes in order to have victory, not only must one seek godly companions, but one must let go of ungodly companions.

Again, wisdom and foolishness in Scripture is not an intellectual issue; it's a moral issue. The fool says in his heart there is no God (Psalm 14:1). The fear of the Lord is the beginning of wisdom (Proverbs 9:10). Choose wise soldiers to fight with—those who are pursuing righteousness out of a pure heart (2 Tim 2:22)—and let go of those who hinder spiritual progress.

In these friendships with the wise, employ the tactics of accountability and prayer. James gives us an anointed prescription for breaking strongholds in the life of a believer. He says, "Therefore confess your sins to each other and pray for each other so that you may be healed. The prayer of a righteous man is powerful and effective" (James 5:16). Though this healing may primarily refer to physical healing caused by sin (cf. James 5:14-15), it no doubt also refers to spiritual healing (cf. James 5:19-20). Personally, through confessing my failures to others and having them pray for me, I have experienced renewed strength for my battles.

Confession of sin both to God and to others is crucial. One of Satan's schemes is encouraging believers to hide sin, instead of confessing it. Through spiritual hypocrisy, strongholds are developed and fortified in a believer's life. This is the kind of Christian that Satan will destroy. They have closet addictions—closet lusts—that they never share with anyone.

When Christians don't confess before God and others, they become desensitized to their sin—opening the door for greater strongholds. Paul talks about false teachers who have a "seared conscience" and are deceived by demons in 1 Timothy 4:1-2. Listen to what he says:

> The Spirit clearly says that in later times some will abandon the faith and follow deceiving spirits and things taught by demons. Such teachings come through hypocritical liars, whose consciences have been seared as with a hot iron.

Paul called them "hypocritical liars"—meaning they professed godliness while living in unconfessed sin. Because of this, their consciences stopped working—making them more susceptible to demonic deception. Living in unconfessed sin opens the door for the devil in our lives.

This happens to Christians all the time. How does a pastor who preaches every week continually steal money from the church and live in an adulterous relationship? This type of stumbling doesn't happen all at once. It's typically a process of living in unrepentant sin while professing godliness. The hypocrisy slowly silences the conscience of the believer and further opens the door for the enemy.

We have all experienced this before. When I was in high school, I struggled with cursing. I would curse during the day, confess my sins at night, and commit to try harder the next day. However, eventually, I could curse and not feel convicted about it at all—I could live in it. By practicing sin, both my conscience and the Holy Spirit were silenced leading to greater sin.

This is what Satan aims to do in the area of sexual immorality. By continually living in unconfessed sexual sin, it opens the door for demonic deception and control, as demonstrated in the false teachers. Believers quickly find themselves bound to pornography addictions, sexual fantasies, homosexual desires, illicit sex, etc. This is the pathway to destruction, and it typically begins with Christians walking alone—with no accountability and confession in their lives.

Solomon, one of the wisest men to ever live, said this:

> Two are better than one, because they have a good return for their work: If one falls down, his friend can help him up. But pity the man who falls and has no one to help him up! Also, if two lie down together, they will keep warm. But how can one keep warm alone? Though one may be overpowered, two can defend themselves. A cord of three strands is not quickly broken.
> Ecclesiastes 4:9-12 (ESV)

"Pity the man who falls and has no one to help him up!" Who are your spiritual warriors who fight beside you? Who picks you up when you fall? Are there strongholds in your life that you haven't confessed to anybody? He who walks with the wise becomes wise—they start to live a victorious, godly life.

This is a strategy every soldier must employ: Find other godly soldiers to fight with—to confess your sins to, to pray with, and to encourage. Also, be willing to let go of those who are not calling on the Lord out of a pure heart.

Reflection

1. Why is it important to have spiritual accountability in the battle for purity?
2. How should one select and initiate an accountability relationship?
3. Who are your accountability partners and how have these relationships helped you?

4. In what ways do worldly friendships and worldly dating relationships lead to suffering harm, especially in the area of sexual purity?
5. What other questions or thoughts do you have about this section?
6. In what ways can you pray in response? Take a second to pray as the Lord leads.

Strategy Eleven: Battle from Home

Whether in sports or war, there is something called home-field advantage. For an athletic team, the home crowd and familiarity with their field or gym gives them a distinct advantage over an opponent. In war, familiarity with the terrain and access to all of one's resources is a tremendous advantage over an enemy.

Living in the world is like living in enemy territory. Satan is the ruler of this world, and therefore, the world culture is immoral. Christians are constantly bombarded with sexual images and suggestive material from every direction. However, though residents of this world, Christians also reside in Christ. It's wonderful to see how Paul expresses this dual residency when talking to the Corinthians. In 1 Corinthians 1:2, he says, "To the church of God that is in Corinth, to those sanctified in Christ Jesus." They are located in Corinth and, at the same time, located in Christ—God. This is where we must war from—our positional relationship with God.

In describing, not so much our war with the world system, but our war with our sinful nature, Paul says, "So I say, live by the Spirit, and you will not gratify the desires of the sinful nature" (Gal 5:16). He says live—make our home—in the Spirit and we will not gratify the desires of the sinful nature. Not only do we have the world attacking us with lust, but we also are attacked from the inside. Our nature lusts after and desires the things of this world. But Paul says that we can have victory if we make our home in the Spirit—our relationship with God.

How do we do this? We do this by doing what the Spirit wants us to do. When we are walking in obedience, meditating daily on God's Word, constantly worshipping, fellowshipping with the saints, and serving God, we will win against our flesh.

Paul describes the fruits of this abiding relationship in Galatians 5:22-23. He says, "But the fruit of the Spirit is love, joy, peace, patience, kindness, goodness, faithfulness, gentleness and self-control. Against such things there is no law." When abiding in the Spirit, one will produce the fruits of the Spirit which includes "self-control"—the ability to control one's lusts.

I have learned to look at my illicit sexual desires this way. If I am struggling with a wandering eye and lust, then it is a warning that I am not living in the Spirit as I should. I look at it as hunger pains. Hunger pains are signals to our brain that it is time to eat. Similarly, we should look at our battle with lust in the same way.

If we are losing this battle, then it is a warning signal for us to increase our time with God—abiding in his Word, prayer, worship, and fellowship. God promises that if we live in the Spirit, we will not satisfy the lust of the flesh. This is a battle that we can win.

Personally, in the early stages of pastoral ministry and marriage, I fell back into a struggle with pornography. One of the ways I dealt with this was by implementing a partial fast into my weekly schedule.

After church on Sunday, about midweek, I always felt more vulnerable—not just to lust but also to depression. Therefore, I started fasting every Wednesday for several years. I would fast until after lunch to allow myself to focus on God. At breakfast and lunch, I would spend more time in the Word and prayer by skipping those meals. During that season, I had to increase my disciplines—making my home in the Spirit—so I would not fulfill the lust of the flesh.

This is true for each of us. God has given us a promise that we can have victory against lust and any other sin if we make our home in the Spirit of God. This can only be done through discipline since we live in a world system that is anti-God and with a flesh that rebels against him as well. We must through discipline make our home in the Spirit—our relationship with God. Paul told Timothy, "discipline yourself unto godliness" (1 Tim 4:7). We must do the same.

Are you fighting from home? If we are not abiding in the Spirit, we will surely abide in sin. There is no middle ground.

Reflection

1. Why is it important for a believer to live in the Spirit when battling lust?
2. What type of disciplines should we practice in order to consistently live in the Spirit? Are there any ways God is calling you to increase those disciplines?
3. How have you experienced losing the battle when not abiding in God?

4. What other questions or thoughts do you have about this section?
5. In what ways can you pray in response? Take a second to pray as the Lord leads.

Strategy Twelve: Declare Victory

Finally, we must understand that we are not fighting to win the battle against lust. The battle has already been won by Christ. We are trying to walk in the victory that Christ already accomplished. This is important to understand because one of Satan's greatest tactics is lying. After a failure, he tells a believer many lies: it is impossible to be free from lust and that he or she will never be a man of God or woman of God.

By accepting lies, we get caught in Satan's trap, and it's easy to become discouraged, defeated, and bound. Jesus said this in John 8:34-36:

> Jesus replied, "I tell you the truth, everyone who sins is a slave to sin. Now a slave has no permanent place in the family, but a son belongs to it forever. So if the Son sets you free, you will be free indeed.

Christ set us free from slavery to sin, and we must understand and appropriate this to walk in victory. Romans 6:6 says, "For we know that our old self was crucified with him so that the body of sin might be done away with, that we should no longer be slaves to sin."

On the cross, Christ did not just pay for our sins; He also broke the power of sin. He took our sin nature and crucified it so we no longer would be slaves to it.

Yes, we can still submit to our sin nature, but we no longer have to because the power of sin has been broken. Like God delivering the Israelites, he not only took them out of Egypt but destroyed the power of Egypt in the Red Sea. Our deliverer, Christ, did no less. We are no longer slaves to sin. However, like Israel, we can still choose to return to Egypt.

How can we walk in this victory? In Romans 6:11, Paul says, "In the same way, count yourselves dead to sin but alive to God in Christ Jesus." The word "count" is an accounting term. This means the debt has been paid, and we are no longer responsible for it. In the same way, Paul says that we are no longer slaves of sin—including our lusts. We owe it no allegiance, and we don't have to obey its cravings. However, we must mentally accept this reality instead of accepting the lies of the devil and our flesh.

Therefore, when Satan tempts us or makes us feel like we have to fall or that we can't get back up after falling, we must recognize that it's all a lie. It's not true! Christ set us free from sin and now we are slaves of righteousness (Romans 6:18). Our allegiance is now to God.

I remember being a young believer and fighting a losing battle to lust. It felt like I would never be free—no matter how much I prayed, fasted, or read my Bible. I felt like a slave—captive to my lust. Understanding Christ's act of abolition on the cross was one of the truths that allowed me to begin to walk in victory.

My bondage to lust was very hard to break. At times, I literally felt like a presence came into my room making me feel overwhelmed and vulnerable in that area. As I reckoned Christ's abolition as true in my life,

I began to fight based on this reality. When I experienced those times of extreme vulnerability, I would stand up and speak out loud what Christ had done for me. I would proclaim, "I am dead to sin; that is not me anymore. I am a slave of righteousness now," and sometimes, I would tell the devil to leave as Christ did when tempted in the wilderness (Matt 4:10).

In my spiritual youth, I didn't fully understand Christ's work on the cross and the extent of what he had done for me. Therefore, I often fought without hope. But now, I fight because the victory has already been won—which gives me great confidence. Christ already defeated Satan and my lust (cf. Col 2:13-15). But, I must reckon this as true (Rom 6:11).

This theological reality is important for many reasons. (1) It means if we stumble, we can get back up. We don't have to accept the lies and condemnation of the devil. Proverbs says the righteous falls seven times and gets back up (Prov 24:16). That's what separates the righteous from the ungodly. They will not stay down. If you have failed in the past, if you failed today, you can start over now because you died to sin with Christ on the cross. Sin no longer identifies you—your identity is in Christ.

(2) But this doctrine is also essential in maintaining our victory. We are no longer slaves of sin but slaves to righteousness. My debt and allegiance is to God. So, I must strive to use the members of my body as instruments of righteousness leading to holiness (Rom 6:13, 19). First Corinthians 6:19-20 says it this way:

> Do you not know that your body is a temple of the Holy Spirit, who is in you, whom you have

received from God? You are not your own; you were bought at a price. Therefore honor God with your body.

We have been bought with a price and are now slaves of God. Therefore, we must faithfully serve God in purity and holiness.

We see the importance of this doctrine in Augustine's walk with God after his conversion. Before Augustine became a Christian, he was very promiscuous. However, at his conversion, everything changed. One day, he ran into a former fling. When he saw her, he turned and ran in the other direction. The lady saw him and was confused. She yelled, "My love! My love! Where are you going? It is I!" He replied, "I know! But it is not I anymore!" and he continued to run away. Augustine recognized this reality—he was not the same. He had been crucified with Christ and he no longer lived—Christ lived within him (Gal 2:20). He was no longer a slave of sin but now a slave of righteousness.

We similarly must reckon this a reality if we are going to walk in victory over lust. We must declare our victory in Christ and walk in it.

Have you declared victory? Or have you declared failure—that you can't win or be free from bondage to lust? If that is you, then you have believed Satan's lie instead of Christ's truth. He who the Son sets free is free indeed (John 8:36). Christ has set you free. Declare your victory and fight to walk in it. Don't give up until your life represents your position in Christ—free from bondage to sin to serve God.

Reflection

1. How did Christ break the power of sin over our lives? Why is understanding this reality—our new identity in Christ—so important to walking in victory?
2. In what ways have you experienced the lies and condemnation of Satan in regards to battling lust?
3. How should we count or reckon our death to lust and freedom from its slavery a reality as Paul teaches (Rom 6:11)?
4. What are the primary strategies from God's Battle Plan for Purity that you feel pressed to implement in your life and/or in mentoring others?
5. What other questions or thoughts do you have about this section?
6. In what ways can you pray in response? Take a second to pray as the Lord leads.

Conclusion

Are you following God's Battle Plan for victory against lust? God's Word equips the man of God for all righteousness (2 Tim 3:16-17). In Scripture, God gives us the strategies to win the battle against lust and to control our body in a way that is pure and honorable, not in lust like the Gentiles (1 Thess 4:3-5). This is not something we know naturally. It is something that must be learned as Paul said. Have you learned how to win the battle against lust? In order to win this battle, we must:

1. Know Our Battle
2. Count the Cost
3. Declare War
4. Guard Our Eyes
5. Guard Our Ears
6. Guard Our Mind
7. Guard Our Free Time
8. Guard Our Brothers and Sisters
9. Guard Our Marriage
10. Find Faithful Soldiers to Fight Beside
11. Battle from Home by Living in the Spirit
12. Declare Victory

Appendix 1

Walking the Romans Road

How can a person be saved? From what is he saved? How can someone have eternal life? Scripture teaches that after death each person will spend eternity either in heaven or hell. How can a person go to heaven?

Paul said this to Timothy:

> But as for you, continue in what you have learned and have become convinced of, because you know those from whom you learned it, and how from infancy you have known the holy Scriptures, which are *able to make you wise for salvation through faith in Christ Jesus.*
> 2 Timothy 3:14-15

One of the reasons God gave us Scripture is to make us wise for salvation. This means that without it nobody can know how to be saved.

Well then, how can a people be saved and what are they being saved from? A common method of sharing the good news of salvation is through the Romans Road. One of the great themes, not only of the Bible, but specifically of the book of Romans is salvation. In Romans, the author, Paul, clearly details the steps we must take in order to be saved.

How can we be saved? What steps must we take?

Step One: We Must Accept that We Are Sinners

Romans 3:23 says, "For all have sinned and fall short of the glory of God." What does it mean to sin? The word sin means "to miss the mark." The mark we missed is looking like God. When God created mankind in the Genesis narrative, he created man in the "image of God" (1:27). The "image of God" means many things, but probably, most importantly it means we were made to be holy just as he is holy. Man was made moral. We were meant to reflect God's holiness in every way: the way we think, the way we talk, and the way we act. And any time we miss the mark in these areas, we commit sin.

Furthermore, we do not only sin when we commit a sinful act such as: lying, stealing, or cheating; again, we sin anytime we have a wrong heart motive. The greatest commandments in Scripture are to "Love God with all our heart, mind, and soul and to love others as ourselves" (Matt 22:36-40, paraphrase). Whenever we don't love God supremely and love others as ourselves, we sin and fall short of the glory of God. For this reason, man is always in a state of sinning. Sadly, even if our actions are good, our heart is bad. I have never loved God with my whole heart, mind, and soul and neither has anybody else. Therefore, we have all sinned and fall short of the glory of God (Rom 3:23). We have all missed the mark of God's holiness and we must accept this.

What's the next step?

Step Two: We Must Understand We Are under the Judgment of God

Why are we under the judgment of God? It is because of our sins. Scripture teaches God is not only a loving God, but he is a just God. And his justice requires judgment for each of our sins. Romans 6:23 says, "For the wages of sin is death."

A wage is something we earn. Every time we sin, we earn the wage of death. What is death? Death really means separation. In physical death, the body is separated from the spirit, but in spiritual death, man is separated from God. Man currently lives in a state of spiritual death (cf. Eph 2:1-3). We do not love God, obey him, or know him as we should. Therefore, man is in a state of death.

Moreover, one day at our physical death, if we have not been saved, we will spend eternity separated from God in a very real hell. In hell, we will pay the wage for each of our sins. Therefore, in hell people will experience various degrees of punishment (cf. Lk 12:47-48). This places man in a very dangerous predicament—unholy and therefore under the judgment of God.

How should we respond to this? This leads us to our third step.

Step Three: We Must Recognize God Has Invited All to Accept His Free Gift of Salvation

Romans 6:23 does not stop at the wages of sin being death. It says, "For the wages of sin is death, but the gift of God is eternal life through Jesus Christ our Lord." Because God loved everybody on the earth, he offered the free gift of eternal life, which anyone can receive through Jesus Christ.

Because it is a gift, it cannot be earned. We cannot work for it. Ephesians 2:8-9 says, "For it is by grace you have been saved, through faith—and this not from yourselves, it is the gift of God—not by works, so that no one can boast."

Going to church, being baptized, giving to the poor, or doing any other righteous work does not save. Salvation is a gift that must be received from God. It is a gift that has been prepared by his effort alone.

How do we receive this free gift?

Step Four: We Must Believe Jesus Christ Died for Our Sins and Rose from the Dead

If we are going to receive this free gift, we must believe in God's Son, Jesus Christ. Because God loved us, cared for us, and didn't want us to be separated from him eternally, he sent his Son to die for our sins. Romans 5:8 says, "But God demonstrates his own love for us in this: While we were still sinners, Christ died for us." Similarly, John 3:16 says, "For God so loved the world that he gave his only begotten son that whosoever believeth in him should not perish but have eternal life." God so loved us that he gave his only Son for our sins.

Jesus Christ was a real, historical person who lived 2,000 years ago. He was born of a virgin. He lived a perfect life. He was put to death by the Romans and the Jews. And he rose again on the third day. In his death, he took our sins and God's wrath for them and gave us his perfect righteousness so we could be accepted by God. Second Corinthians 5:21 says, "God made him who had no sin to be sin for us, so that in him we might become the righteousness of God." God did all this so we could be saved from his wrath.

Christ's death satisfied the just anger of God over our sins. When God saw Jesus on the cross, he saw us and our sins and therefore judged Jesus. And now, when God sees those who are saved, he sees his righteous Son and accepts us. In salvation, we have become the righteousness of God.

If we are going to be saved, if we are going to receive this free gift of salvation, we must believe in Christ's death, burial, and resurrection for our sins (cf. 1 Cor 15:3-5, Rom 10:9-10). Do you believe?

Step Five: We Must Confess Christ as Lord of Our Lives

Romans 10:9-10 says,

> That if you confess with your mouth, "Jesus is Lord," and believe in your heart that God raised him from the dead, you will be saved. For it is with your heart that you believe and are justified, and it is with your mouth that you confess and are saved.

Not only must we believe, but we must confess Christ as Lord of our lives. It is one thing to believe in Christ but another thing to follow Christ. Simple belief does not save. Christ must be our Lord. James said this: "Even the demons believe and shudder" (James 2:19) but the demons are not saved—Christ is not their Lord.

Another aspect of making Christ Lord is *repentance*. Repentance really means a change of mind that leads to a change of direction. Before we met Christ, we were living our own life and following our own sinful desires. But when we get saved, our mind and direction change. We start to follow Christ as Lord.

How do we make this commitment to the lordship of Christ so we can be saved? Paul said we must confess with our mouth "Jesus is Lord" as we believe in him. Romans 10:13 says, "Everyone who calls on the name of the Lord will be saved."

If you admit that you are a sinner and understand you are under God's wrath because of them; if you believe Jesus Christ is the Son of God, that he died on the cross for your sins, and rose from the dead for your salvation; if you are ready to turn from your sin and cling to Christ as Lord, you can be saved.

If this is your heart, then you can pray this prayer and commit to following Christ as your Lord.

> *Dear heavenly Father, I confess I am a sinner and have fallen short of your glory, what you made me for. I believe Jesus Christ died on the cross to pay the penalty for my sins and rose from the dead so I can have eternal life. I am turning away from my sin and accepting you as my Lord and Savior. Come into my life and change me. Thank you for your gift of salvation.*

Scripture teaches that if you truly accepted Christ as your Lord, then you are a new creation. Second Corinthians 5:17 says, "Therefore, if anyone is in Christ, he is a new creation; the old has gone, the new has come!" God has forgiven your sins (1 John

1:9), he has given you his Holy Spirit (Rom 8:15), and he is going to disciple you and make you into the image of his Son (cf. Rom 8:29). He will never leave you nor forsake you (Heb 13:5), and he will complete the work he has begun in your life (Phil 1:6). In heaven, angels and saints are rejoicing because of your commitment to Christ (Lk 15:7).

Praise God for his great salvation! May God keep you in his hand, empower you through the Holy Spirit, train you through mature believers, and use you to build his kingdom! "The one who calls you is faithful, he will do it" (1 Thess 5:24). God bless you!

Coming Soon

Praise the Lord for your interest in studying and teaching God's Word. If God has blessed you through the BTG series, please partner with us in petitioning God to greatly use this series to encourage and build his Church. Also, please consider leaving an Amazon review. By doing this, you help spread the "Word." Thanks for your partnership in the gospel from the first day until now (Phil 1:4-5).

Available:
First Peter
Theology Proper
Building Foundations for a Godly Marriage
Colossians
God's Battle Plan for Purity
Nehemiah

Coming Soon:
Philippians
Abraham
Ephesians

About the Author

Greg Brown earned his MA in religion and MA in teaching from Trinity International University, a MRE from Liberty University, and a PhD in theology from Louisiana Baptist University. He has served over ten years in pastoral ministry and currently serves as Chaplain and Assistant Professor at Handong Global University, pastor at Handong International Congregation, and as a Navy Reserve chaplain.

Greg married his lovely wife Tara Jayne in 2006, and they have one daughter, Saiyah Grace. He enjoys going on dates with his wife, playing with his daughter, reading, writing, studying in coffee shops, working out, and following the NBA and UFC. His pursuit in life, simply stated, is "to know God and to be found faithful by Him."

To connect with Greg, please follow at http://www.pgregbrown.com.

Notes

[1] Accessed 8/25/2015 from http://ancienthistory.about.com/cs/sexuality/a/aa011400a.htm
[2] Accessed 8/25/2015 from http://www.dailyinfographic.com/the-stats-on-internet-pornography-infographic
[3] Accessed 8/25/2015 from http://www.covenanteyes.com/pornstats/
[4] Accessed 8/28/2015 from http://www.woar.org/resources/sexual-assault-statistics.php
[5] Accessed 8/28/2015 from https://rainn.org/statistics
[6] Accessed 8/25/ 2015 from http://biblehub.com/topical/s/simple.htm
[7] Wiegel, Robert, "How Does God's Word Change Us." Sermon accessed 8/25/2015 from https://sermons.logos.com/submissions/49039-19-Psalm-019-7-08-How-Does-Gods-Word-Change-Us#content=/submissions/49039
[8] MacArthur, J. F., Jr. (1986). *Ephesians* (p. 222). Chicago: Moody Press.

www.ingramcontent.com/pod-product-compliance
Lightning Source LLC
Chambersburg PA
CBHW061338040426
42444CB00011B/2979